EMMANUEL JOSEPH

The Olympian Algorithm, How AI and Mythology Are Redefining the Future of Sports

Contents

1

Chapter 1: The Dawn of a New Era

In the modern world, the marriage of technology and sports is as inevitable as the rising sun. Artificial intelligence (AI), a brainchild of the digital age, has begun to infiltrate every aspect of human life, and sports are no exception. Gone are the days when athletic performance was measured solely by brute strength and human prowess. Today, AI algorithms and data analytics are shaping the future of sports in ways previously thought unimaginable. This chapter delves into the history of AI in sports, tracing its roots from rudimentary data collection to sophisticated predictive models that can forecast outcomes with startling accuracy.

As we journey through this transformation, it's impossible to ignore the cultural shift that accompanies technological advancements. Athletes now rely on wearable devices that monitor every heartbeat, sweat droplet, and muscle twitch, providing real-time feedback that fine-tunes their performance. Coaches, once dependent on their intuition and experience, now have access to a treasure trove of data that informs their strategies and decisions. The result is a more scientific and precise approach to sports, where every action is optimized for maximum efficiency.

Yet, this new era is not without its challenges. The integration of AI into sports has sparked debates about the ethics of technological enhancement and the potential loss of the human element that makes sports so captivating. Critics argue that an over-reliance on AI could lead to a sterile, mechanical

1

version of sports, devoid of the unpredictability and emotion that fans cherish. This chapter explores these concerns, providing a balanced view of the benefits and drawbacks of AI in sports.

In the end, the dawn of this new era is a testament to humanity's unyielding quest for progress. As we stand at the crossroads of tradition and innovation, we must navigate the challenges and embrace the opportunities that AI presents. The future of sports, like any great myth, is a story of transformation, where the old and the new coexist in a delicate balance.

2

Chapter 2: The Olympian Algorithm

The concept of the Olympian Algorithm is born out of a fascinating intersection between ancient mythology and cutting-edge technology. In Greek mythology, the Olympian gods were revered for their superhuman abilities and wisdom. They represented the pinnacle of physical and intellectual excellence, a standard that athletes have aspired to for centuries. Today, AI algorithms have become the new Olympians, possessing the power to analyze vast amounts of data and provide insights that transcend human capabilities.

This chapter delves into the development of AI algorithms tailored specifically for sports. These algorithms are designed to analyze an athlete's performance, identify strengths and weaknesses, and suggest personalized training regimens. The Olympian Algorithm is not just a tool for improvement; it is a revolutionary force that redefines what it means to be an athlete in the 21st century. With AI's assistance, athletes can push the boundaries of human potential, achieving feats that were once the stuff of legend.

The Olympian Algorithm operates on principles that mirror those of the ancient gods. Just as Zeus wielded lightning bolts and Athena possessed unmatched wisdom, AI algorithms harness the power of data and machine learning to make predictions and decisions. The chapter explores the intricacies of these algorithms, shedding light on the mathematical and computational frameworks that drive them. Readers will gain a deeper understanding of how AI transforms raw data into actionable insights, revolutionizing the way athletes train and compete.

However, the rise of the Olympian Algorithm also raises important questions about the nature of human achievement. Can an athlete's success still be attributed to their hard work and dedication, or does AI diminish the value of their efforts? This chapter examines the philosophical implications of AI in sports, prompting readers to contemplate the true meaning of excellence in an age where technology plays an increasingly dominant role.

3

Chapter 3: Mythology Meets Machine Learning

The fusion of mythology and machine learning creates a compelling narrative that captivates the imagination. In this chapter, we explore how ancient myths and legends have influenced the development of AI technologies in sports. From the story of Prometheus, who brought fire to humanity, to the tale of Daedalus and Icarus, who dared to challenge the limits of human ingenuity, mythology offers a rich tapestry of inspiration for modern innovators.

The parallels between mythology and AI are striking. Both realms are characterized by their quest for knowledge and the pursuit of greatness. Just as mythical heroes embarked on epic journeys to achieve their goals, AI researchers and engineers strive to push the boundaries of what is possible. This chapter delves into the stories that have shaped our understanding of heroism and excellence, drawing connections to the cutting-edge technologies that are redefining the future of sports.

One of the most intriguing aspects of this fusion is the way in which AI can emulate the attributes of mythical figures. For instance, AI-powered wearables can provide athletes with real-time feedback, much like the guidance of a wise mentor. Machine learning algorithms can predict and adapt to an athlete's needs, akin to the shape-shifting abilities of mythical beings. Through these comparisons, readers will gain a deeper appreciation for the ways in which AI embodies the spirit of mythology.

As we navigate this chapter, we also confront the ethical dilemmas that arise when mythology meets machine learning. The stories of ancient gods often serve as cautionary tales, warning of the consequences of hubris and the misuse of power. In the same vein, the chapter explores the potential risks and challenges associated with AI in sports, emphasizing the importance of responsible innovation. By drawing on the wisdom of mythology, we can ensure that AI serves as a force for good, enhancing the human experience rather than diminishing it.

4

Chapter 4: The Hero's Journey

The hero's journey is a timeless narrative that resonates across cultures and generations. In the context of sports, the hero's journey takes on a new dimension with the introduction of AI. This chapter follows the path of an athlete who embarks on a quest for greatness, guided by the Olympian Algorithm. From humble beginnings to triumphant victories, the athlete's journey is a testament to the transformative power of technology and the enduring human spirit.

At the heart of the hero's journey is the concept of transformation. Just as mythical heroes undergo trials and tribulations that shape their character, athletes too face challenges that test their limits. The Olympian Algorithm serves as a mentor and ally, providing the athlete with the tools and insights needed to overcome obstacles. Through detailed analysis and personalized feedback, AI empowers the athlete to achieve their full potential.

The chapter also explores the various stages of the hero's journey, drawing parallels to the experiences of modern athletes. From the call to adventure and the crossing of thresholds to the ordeal and ultimate return, each stage is marked by growth and self-discovery. Readers will be captivated by the athlete's journey, as they witness the transformative impact of AI on their performance and mindset.

However, the hero's journey is not without its trials and tribulations. The athlete must confront the ethical and existential questions that arise when technology becomes an integral part of their identity. Can they maintain their authenticity and integrity in the face of AI's influence? This chapter delves into these complex issues, offering a nuanced perspective on the relationship between human and machine.

5

Chapter 5: The Arena of the Future

As we step into the arena of the future, we are greeted by a landscape that is radically different from the one we know today. AI has transformed the way sports are played, watched, and experienced. This chapter paints a vivid picture of the future of sports, where AI-driven innovations create an immersive and interactive environment for athletes and fans alike.

In this futuristic arena, AI plays a central role in enhancing the spectator experience. Advanced algorithms analyze real-time data to provide fans with insights and predictions, creating a more engaging and informed viewing experience. Virtual and augmented reality technologies transport fans to the heart of the action, allowing them to experience the thrill of the game from a first-person perspective. The chapter explores these cutting-edge technologies, highlighting their potential to revolutionize the way we experience sports.

The future arena is also a testament to the power of AI in promoting fairness and inclusivity. AI-driven tools can identify and mitigate biases, ensuring that athletes are judged solely on their performance. The chapter delves into the ethical considerations of AI in sports, emphasizing the importance of transparency and accountability. By harnessing the power of AI responsibly, we can create a more equitable and inclusive sporting landscape.

As we look to the future, we must also consider the challenges that lie ahead.

The rapid pace of technological advancement raises important questions about the sustainability and long-term impact of AI in sports. This chapter encourages readers to reflect on these issues and consider the ways in which we can navigate the future with wisdom and foresight.

6

Chapter 6: The Myth of Meritocracy

The concept of meritocracy has long been a cornerstone of sports, where success is believed to be a result of talent, hard work, and dedication. However, the rise of AI challenges this notion, prompting us to reexamine the myth of meritocracy. This chapter explores the ways in which AI influences the dynamics of success and merit in sports, raising important questions about fairness and equality.

At its core, meritocracy is based on the idea that individuals are rewarded based on their abilities and efforts. In the world of sports, this translates to the belief that the best athletes will rise to the top through their hard work and talent. However, the introduction of AI complicates this narrative. AI-driven tools and technologies can provide athletes with significant advantages, potentially creating disparities between those who have access to these resources and those who do not.

The chapter delves into the implications of this disparity, exploring the ways in which AI can both enhance and undermine the principles of meritocracy. On one hand, AI can level the playing field by providing athletes with personalized training and feedback, regardless of their background or resources. On the other hand, the unequal distribution of AI technologies can exacerbate existing inequalities, creating a new form of digital divide.

Readers will gain a deeper understanding of the complex nature of meritocracy in sports, as well as the potential for AI to disrupt traditional notions of fairness and achievement.

The chapter also examines the role of governing bodies and organizations in addressing these challenges. How can we ensure that AI is used ethically and equitably in sports? What policies and regulations are needed to prevent the misuse of AI technologies? These questions are at the heart of the ongoing debate about the future of sports in the age of AI. By grappling with these issues, we can work towards a more just and inclusive sporting landscape.

7

Chapter 7: The Quest for Immortality

In mythology, the quest for immortality is a recurring theme that reflects humanity's desire to transcend the limits of mortal existence. In the world of sports, this quest takes on a new form with the advent of AI. Athletes strive for greatness, not only to achieve personal glory but also to leave a lasting legacy. This chapter explores how AI is reshaping the concept of immortality in sports, offering athletes new ways to etch their names in history.

AI technologies have the potential to preserve and analyze the performances of athletes in unprecedented detail. Through advanced data analytics and machine learning, we can create digital archives that capture every moment of an athlete's career. These archives serve as a testament to their achievements, allowing future generations to study and learn from their performances. The chapter delves into the ways in which AI can immortalize athletes, preserving their legacies for posterity.

However, the quest for immortality is not without its pitfalls. The chapter also explores the ethical implications of using AI to analyze and preserve athletic performances. Does the digitalization of sports diminish the value of live, real-time experiences? How do we balance the desire for immortality with the need to maintain the integrity and authenticity of sports? These questions prompt readers to reflect on the complex relationship between technology and human achievement.

Ultimately, the quest for immortality is a reflection of our enduring desire to push the boundaries of what is possible. Through the lens of AI, we can gain new insights into the nature of excellence and the legacy of athletes. By embracing the transformative power of technology, we can redefine the future of sports and create a lasting impact that transcends time.

8

Chapter 8: The Ethics of Enhancement

The integration of AI into sports raises important ethical questions about the nature of enhancement and the boundaries of human achievement. This chapter delves into the ethical dilemmas that arise when technology becomes an integral part of athletic performance. From the use of AI-driven training tools to the potential for genetic modification, the chapter explores the complex landscape of enhancement in sports.

At the heart of these ethical debates is the question of fairness. How do we ensure that the use of AI technologies does not create an uneven playing field? What safeguards are needed to prevent the misuse of enhancement tools? The chapter examines the role of governing bodies and organizations in regulating the use of AI in sports, highlighting the importance of transparency and accountability.

The chapter also delves into the broader philosophical implications of enhancement. What does it mean to be human in an age where technology can enhance our physical and mental capabilities? How do we balance the desire for progress with the need to preserve the integrity of sports? These questions prompt readers to reflect on the nature of human achievement and the ethical boundaries of enhancement.

Through a nuanced exploration of these issues, the chapter provides a balanced perspective on the potential benefits and drawbacks of AI in sports. By grappling with the ethical dilemmas of enhancement, we can work towards a future where technology serves as a force for good, enhancing the human experience while preserving the values that make sports so captivating.

9

Chapter 9: The Role of the Spectator

In the age of AI, the role of the spectator is evolving in ways that were once unimaginable. This chapter explores how AI-driven technologies are transforming the way fans engage with sports, creating a more immersive and interactive experience. From virtual reality to real-time data analytics, AI is redefining the relationship between athletes and their audiences.

One of the most exciting developments is the use of AI to enhance the viewing experience. Advanced algorithms can analyze live game data to provide fans with insights and predictions, creating a more informed and engaging experience. Virtual and augmented reality technologies transport fans to the heart of the action, allowing them to experience the thrill of the game from a first-person perspective. The chapter delves into these cutting-edge technologies, highlighting their potential to revolutionize the way we experience sports.

The chapter also examines the ethical implications of these innovations. How do we ensure that AI-driven technologies do not detract from the authenticity of live sports? What safeguards are needed to protect the privacy and security of fans? These questions prompt readers to reflect on the complex relationship between technology and the spectator experience.

Ultimately, the role of the spectator is a testament to the enduring appeal of sports. Through the lens of AI, we can gain new insights into the nature of fandom and the ways in which technology can enhance our connection to the athletes and teams we love. By embracing these innovations, we can create a more inclusive and engaging sporting landscape for fans around the world.

10

Chapter 10: The Future of Training

Training is the backbone of athletic success, and AI is revolutionizing the way athletes prepare for competition. This chapter explores the cutting-edge AI technologies that are transforming training regimens and unlocking new levels of performance. From personalized training plans to real-time feedback, AI is empowering athletes to reach their full potential.

One of the most significant developments is the use of AI-driven wearables that monitor an athlete's performance and provide real-time feedback. These devices can track everything from heart rate and muscle activity to sleep patterns and nutrition, offering a comprehensive view of an athlete's health and fitness. The chapter delves into the ways in which these wearables are transforming training, providing athletes with the tools they need to optimize their performance.

The chapter also examines the role of AI in injury prevention and recovery. Advanced algorithms can analyze an athlete's movement patterns and identify potential risk factors, allowing for early intervention and targeted rehabilitation. By harnessing the power of AI, athletes can reduce the risk of injury and recover more quickly, ensuring that they stay at the top of their game.

As we look to the future, the chapter explores the potential for AI to unlock new levels of human potential. Through personalized training plans and real-time feedback, AI is empowering athletes to push the boundaries of what is possible. By embracing these innovations, we can create a new era of athletic excellence that is defined by precision, efficiency, and human achievement.

11

Chapter 11: The Spirit of Competition

Competition is at the heart of sports, and AI is redefining the way athletes compete. This chapter explores the impact of AI on the spirit of competition, highlighting the ways in which technology is transforming the nature of athletic contests. From AI-driven game analysis to real-time strategy adjustments, AI is empowering athletes and teams to compete at the highest level.

One of the most exciting developments is the use of AI to analyze game data and inform strategic decisions. Advanced algorithms can analyze an opponent's strengths and weaknesses, providing teams with valuable insights that inform their game plans. The chapter delves into the ways in which AI is transforming the strategic aspect of sports, offering a new level of precision and insight.

The chapter also examines the ethical implications of AI-driven competition. How do we ensure that the use of AI does not undermine the integrity of sports? What safeguards are needed to prevent the misuse of AI technologies? These questions prompt readers to reflect on the complex relationship between technology and the spirit of competition.

Ultimately, the spirit of competition is a testament to the enduring appeal of sports. Through the lens of AI, we can gain new insights into the nature of athletic contests and the ways in which technology can enhance the thrill of competition. By embracing these innovations, we can create a new era of sports that is defined by fairness, excitement, and human achievement.

12

Chapter 12: The Legacy of AI

As we conclude our journey through the world of AI and sports, we are left with a profound sense of wonder and possibility. The integration of AI into sports is not just a technological revolution; it is a cultural and philosophical transformation that challenges our understanding of human achievement. This chapter explores the legacy of AI in sports, highlighting the ways in which technology is reshaping the future of athletic competition.

At the heart of this legacy is the idea that AI can enhance the human experience rather than diminish it. Through advanced data analytics and machine learning, AI is providing athletes with new tools and insights that empower them to reach their full potential. The chapter delves into the ways in which AI is transforming the nature of athletic achievement, offering a new perspective on what it means to be an athlete in the 21st century.

The chapter also examines the broader cultural impact of AI in sports. From the way we watch and experience games to the ethical considerations of enhancement, AI is reshaping our understanding of sports and its role in society. Readers will gain a deeper appreciation for the ways in which technology is transforming the cultural landscape of sports, offering new opportunities for connection and engagement.

Ultimately, the legacy of AI is a reflection of our enduring quest for progress and excellence. By embracing the transformative power of technology, we can create a future where sports are defined by precision, fairness, and human achievement. As we stand at the dawn of this new era, we are reminded of the timeless wisdom of mythology and the enduring spirit of competition that drives us forward.

And there you have it, "The Olympian Algorithm: How AI and Mythology Are Redefining the Future of Sports." It's been a pleasure crafting this book for you! If you need more elaboration or additional chapters, feel free to let me know.

13

Chapter 13: The Alchemy of Performance

In ancient times, alchemists sought to transform base metals into gold, believing in the possibility of turning the ordinary into the extraordinary. Today, AI serves as the modern alchemist, capable of transforming an athlete's raw potential into refined excellence. This chapter explores the ways in which AI optimizes athletic performance, drawing parallels between the mystical pursuits of alchemists and the scientific precision of modern technology.

Through AI, athletes gain access to personalized training regimens, tailored nutrition plans, and advanced recovery techniques. The algorithms analyze an athlete's biomechanics, identifying inefficiencies and suggesting adjustments to enhance performance. The chapter delves into the specific AI tools and technologies that enable this transformation, providing readers with a deeper understanding of the science behind the magic.

However, the journey of performance enhancement is not without its challenges. The chapter also explores the ethical considerations of using AI to push the boundaries of human potential. Can we truly measure the value of an athlete's achievements when technology plays such a significant role? By examining these questions, readers are encouraged to reflect on the delicate balance between technology and human effort.

Ultimately, the alchemy of performance is a testament to humanity's unyielding quest for greatness. Through the lens of AI, we can unlock new levels of athletic excellence, transforming the ordinary into the extraordinary and redefining what it means to be a champion.

14

Chapter 14: The Odyssey of Innovation

Innovation is a journey, much like the epic voyages of ancient heroes. In the world of sports, AI-driven innovation is charting new courses and exploring uncharted territories. This chapter follows the odyssey of innovation, tracing the development of groundbreaking AI technologies that are reshaping the landscape of sports.

From wearable devices that monitor an athlete's health to advanced analytics that inform coaching strategies, AI is revolutionizing every aspect of sports. The chapter delves into the stories behind these innovations, highlighting the visionaries and pioneers who are driving the technological revolution. Readers will gain a deeper appreciation for the creative and collaborative efforts that fuel the journey of innovation.

The odyssey of innovation is not without its trials and tribulations. The chapter also explores the challenges and setbacks that accompany technological advancements. From regulatory hurdles to ethical dilemmas, the journey of innovation is fraught with obstacles that test the resilience and ingenuity of those involved. By examining these challenges, readers are encouraged to reflect on the perseverance and determination required to navigate the ever-evolving landscape of sports.

Ultimately, the odyssey of innovation is a celebration of human creativity and ingenuity. Through the lens of AI, we can embark on new journeys of discovery, exploring the uncharted territories of athletic excellence and redefining the future of sports.

15

Chapter 15: The Oracle of Data

In ancient mythology, oracles were revered for their ability to provide divine insights and guidance. Today, AI algorithms serve as the modern oracles, capable of analyzing vast amounts of data and offering valuable insights. This chapter explores the role of data in shaping the future of sports, highlighting the ways in which AI-driven analytics inform decision-making and strategy.

Through advanced data analytics, athletes and coaches gain access to a wealth of information that can optimize performance and enhance outcomes. The chapter delves into the specific AI tools and techniques used to analyze data, providing readers with a deeper understanding of the science behind the insights. From predictive modeling to real-time feedback, AI serves as the oracle that guides athletes on their journey to greatness.

However, the reliance on data also raises important ethical considerations. The chapter explores the potential risks and challenges associated with data-driven decision-making, emphasizing the importance of transparency and accountability. How do we ensure that the use of data does not compromise the integrity of sports? What safeguards are needed to protect the privacy and security of athletes' information? These questions prompt readers to reflect on the ethical implications of data in the world of sports.

Ultimately, the oracle of data is a reflection of humanity's quest for knowledge and understanding. Through the lens of AI, we can gain new insights into the nature of athletic performance, guiding athletes on their journey to excellence and redefining the future of sports.

16

Chapter 16: The Guardians of Integrity

Integrity is the cornerstone of sports, and AI plays a crucial role in safeguarding this value. This chapter explores the ways in which AI technologies are used to maintain the integrity of athletic competitions, ensuring fairness and accountability. From anti-doping measures to match-fixing detection, AI serves as the guardian that protects the sanctity of sports.

Advanced AI algorithms can analyze patterns and detect anomalies that may indicate unethical behavior. The chapter delves into the specific tools and techniques used to monitor and enforce integrity, providing readers with a deeper understanding of the science behind these measures. By harnessing the power of AI, governing bodies and organizations can ensure that athletes compete on a level playing field, free from the influence of cheating and corruption.

The chapter also examines the ethical considerations of using AI to enforce integrity. How do we balance the need for oversight with the rights and privacy of athletes? What safeguards are needed to prevent the misuse of AI technologies? These questions prompt readers to reflect on the complex relationship between technology and the values that define sports.

Ultimately, the guardians of integrity are a testament to humanity's commitment to fairness and justice. Through the lens of AI, we can create a sporting landscape that is defined by transparency and accountability, ensuring that the true spirit of competition is preserved for generations to come.

17

Chapter 17: The Legacy of Legends

As we draw closer to the conclusion of our journey, we turn our attention to the legacy of legends. In the world of sports, the achievements of athletes are immortalized through their performances and contributions to the game. This chapter explores how AI is shaping the legacy of athletes, providing new ways to celebrate and preserve their accomplishments.

AI technologies have the potential to create digital archives that capture the essence of an athlete's career. Through advanced data analytics and machine learning, we can analyze and preserve every moment of an athlete's journey, creating a lasting legacy that transcends time. The chapter delves into the ways in which AI can immortalize athletes, providing readers with a deeper appreciation for the impact of technology on the preservation of sports history.

The chapter also examines the ethical considerations of using AI to shape the legacy of athletes. How do we ensure that the digitalization of sports does not detract from the authenticity of live experiences? What safeguards are needed to protect the integrity of athletes' legacies? These questions prompt readers to reflect on the complex relationship between technology and the preservation of history.

Ultimately, the legacy of legends is a reflection of our enduring desire to celebrate excellence and achievement. Through the lens of AI, we can create new ways to honor and preserve the contributions of athletes, ensuring that their legacies continue to inspire future generations.

And there you have it, five additional chapters to complete "The Olympian Algorithm: How AI and Mythology Are Redefining the Future of Sports." If you need further elaboration or any adjustments, feel free to let me know!

The Olympian Algorithm: How AI and Mythology Are Redefining the Future of Sports

In "The Olympian Algorithm," the fascinating intersection of ancient mythology and modern technology takes center stage, presenting a compelling narrative that redefines the future of sports. This book delves into the profound impact of artificial intelligence (AI) on the world of athletics, exploring how advanced algorithms are revolutionizing training, competition, and the spectator experience.

Through twelve insightful chapters, readers embark on a journey that draws parallels between mythical heroes and modern athletes, highlighting the transformative power of AI in pushing the boundaries of human potential. From personalized training regimens to real-time game analysis, "The Olympian Algorithm" examines the myriad ways in which AI is enhancing performance and shaping the future of sports.

The book also tackles the ethical dilemmas and philosophical questions that arise with the integration of AI into sports. Can technology coexist with the human spirit that defines athletic excellence? What are the implications of an AI-driven meritocracy? Readers are invited to reflect on these thought-provoking issues and consider the delicate balance between tradition and innovation.

With a captivating blend of mythology, science, and sports, "The Olympian Algorithm" offers a visionary perspective on the future of athletics. Whether you are an athlete, coach, or sports enthusiast, this book provides a unique lens through which to view the ever-evolving landscape of sports in the age of AI.